this is the alphabet now

haiku, senryu, haiga/visual poems

Jean LeBlanc

Copyright© 2025 Jean LeBlanc
ISBN: 978-93-6354-599-1

First Edition: 2025
Rs. 250/-

Cyberwit.net
HIG 45 Kaushambi Kunj, Kalindipuram
Allahabad - 211011 (U.P.) India
http://www.cyberwit.net
E-mail: info@cyberwit.net

No part of this book may be reproduced or transmitted in any form or by any means, electronic, mechanical, photocopying, or otherwise, without the express written consent of Jean LeBlanc.

Printed at Repro India Limited.

ACKNOWLEDGMENTS

Some of these poems have appeared in *tinywords*, *password*, and *World Haiku*. I am deeply grateful to the editors of these journals.

More so than ever before, for George.

haiku: smooth river stones
senryu: stream in a culvert

haiku: oak and moon
senryu: scissors and glue

green mountains greener
you take my hand

turning the page
pieces of me
become whole

lost river
childhood memories
gone underground

a verse so small violets loom

he whispers into my deaf ear
i read his eyes

spring alphabet
on the forest floor
crushed by so little snow

ice cave
as if we've never said
these words before

the alphabet
what we know
of dark matter

harp moon, hope moon
the world without my glasses

enough sinkholes and you only have valley

such a ruckus
all this talk
about cicadas

surgery prep
watching the kite festival
on tv

vulture syllables
your anthology
of blank pages

thruway exit
a red-tailed's sudden
u-turn

before the alphabet a killing frost

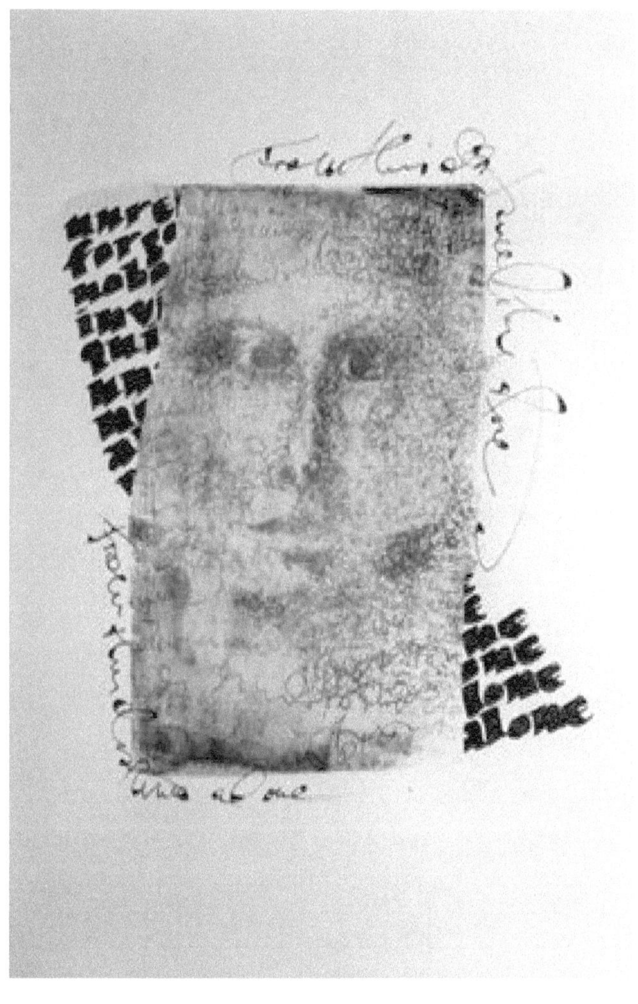

today's journal page
in place of a date
a crow

november hyperbole
a hawk
in every tree

skyline mudflat heron skyflat mudline here on

museum lighting
Degas's little dancer
casts twin shadows

Christina's world—
my student says
she lives next door

museum field trip admiring all the frames

wedding anniversary—
a note reminding me
to turn up the heat

late autumn—
three vultures wait all morning
for an updraft

post-op instructions
my husband helps me
water the marigolds

spring ephemerals bird no bird

yellow violet, white indigo
oxymorons all in bloom

news clipping
how quickly the past
turns brittle

tie-dyed tees
the casual injustice
of long ago

rhetoric and critique
trying to get a question
to my answer

crows back and forth
dumpster heist in progress

no more sunrise—
the big lake strafed
with powerlines

the abandoned dock
where swallows
raise their young

call it 'lake'
call it 'pond'
turtle dances with turtle

your home alphabet
science
sword
silence

word puzzles
not fully present
at this meeting

insomnia
the foggy morning
lasts all day

hem   ming   haw   ing
an answer   at last
maybe?

empty-handed
life line and money line
both broken

Greylock's silhouette —
every night in Melville's dreams
the whale

blueberry by
[making our way up Noonmark]
blueberry

drowning in the alphabet
we do not agree

ankle surgery
all shoes
someone else's shoes

waterlily close-up my sneakers fill with lake

wedding reception my shoes older than the groom

every year, this poem—
explaining to my students
what shoe trees are

lilacs early this year
i miss my mother's birthday

cinnamon water
in the microwave—
pretending i bake

magnolia's
farewell
petal
by
p
e
t
a
l

strawberry rhubarb
some marriages just work

hot cross buns
another holiday
i've outgrown

sharp-edged dune grass
adults arguing
against the wind

saltmarsh at low tide
our last new bird together

on any random page
crows

yesterday's high tide
a wavy line of broken shells

little blue heron
and that's why our gods and our lives

poetry translates into authority
but only with this pen

the bell for recess—
a whole new set
of rules

half-wild
in my mother's garden
bellflowers

the alphabet now—
the council becomes a sword

home from the road trip
with a mile-long list
of birds

car camping
two pup tents
in a sea of RVs

country squire my father's last car

pull-off at the top
of Breakneck Road—
the radiator's time-out

not enough warning, juncos—
the bell on the cat's collar

            perfect
      a   hill
   curve   for
bell   sledding

the phrase is served its due

thirty years now
the same carousel horses
still going strong

processing these words
the option to undo

kigo on my computer screen—
for half the world, it's summer

all her memories shift control delete

heron screen saver
the virtual present

arguing until the shape of birds

polished floors
my stories
wander off

prec [i] se folds or [i] gam [i]

smooth stones
along the riverbank
one of us turns mean

sketching the river
indoors warm and dry

slate roof
covering what long ago
collapsed

snow moon
the familiar stomach ache
of sunday

become calligraphy
become the tendrils
between words

its own verb rain
its own noun gray

junk journal
a list of places
i'll never

homestead
the well full
of trash

pied and motley
these playing cards
predict the present

solitaire
you win
the joker says

because your name is synonymous with thorn

every light in the house it takes more than that

he died last year the stepping stones reset

song or call red-winged blackbird in between

midstream stopping to break the sun

your footbridge promise your ice age tricks

in this ravine
the relative merits
of lichen and fern

what to make of the news
loons on their way north

sheltering in place—
so far away
the grave they share

verb tense but aren't we all

sunrise a little like our plans on hold

on her headstone
her lifelong wish—
her name spelled correctly

mudflats at low tide
our last new bird together

curvature of spine
her body the alphabet
of lonely

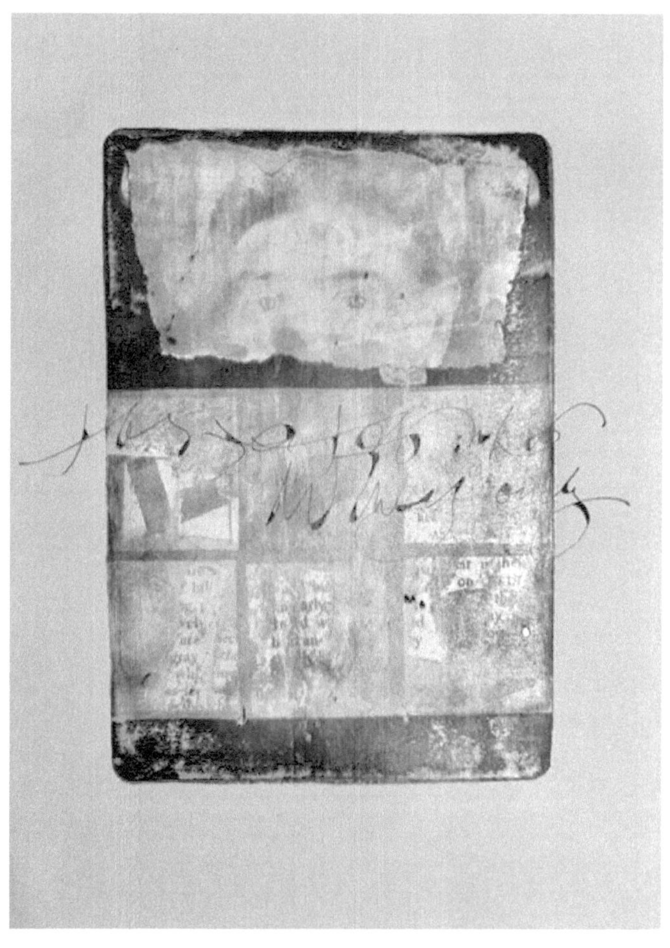

autumn breeze
so many moons
in the river

once a phlox garden
now the wind hardly matters

another blood test
another winter that won't let go

your first full moon
as well as your last
dragonfly

spring garden
every few seconds
an umbrella opens

moonset soaked through with dew

summer all at once
the first few notes
of a song he hates

after the storm
in our little railroad town
painted bunting

false foxglove
a hummingbird unconcerned
with common names

a lull in the pull of the moon is all

pall bearers the coffin full of gall

prayer or paper
both take the color well

blue transfer
shards in a new-ploughed field

quiet valley but what if a voice rings out

hard-packed ground
nothing to do but pity
the roots

tendril and curl
this is the alphabet now

what did you mean
(the translator doesn't respond)

alphabet in pieces
the translators all
on strike

my mother again
the turned-down corners
of my mouth

corn moon
not even a kernel
of truth

mar the marrow
the calendar contracts

always the wrong blue
wrong green
the only palette there is

four-way stop
every driver
waves

the doll whose eyes could blink
also the one who could speak

first time here since—
no one has much
to say

winter sun
all day long
these walking silhouettes

haiku workshop
laughing at how often
we get mooned

river's course/curse
to flow through
this town

double helix
my clumsy feet
on these spiral stairs

closed caption typo
'the money's all gown'

throwing a pot
her hands formed
from the same clay

other mill towns, fine—
just not the one
where i was born

wren—
there is no word
there is no in the world

civic improvements
trying to make the river
smell like river

the weight on
her shoulders
juvenilia

follows me from pillow to tea nightmare

elegant tendrils
the nape
of her handwriting

splatter of ink
five new stars in the universe

solitude
the sacrilege
of guzzling tea

 it's all here
last year's leaves
this year's tulips

nature walk
so little time
for sparrows

beneath live oaks
fresh plastic flowers
for his grave

wife of
[and here the stone
is broken]

goldenrod bouquet
a bee tapping
at the window

the notebook
on the far side
of the moon

yesterday's crows
just when we think
we're all out of tears

cannot take this curve without egret

saluting the sky
hoping the crows
remember

picking an alphabet
from the snow-crushed reeds

www.ingramcontent.com/pod-product-compliance
Lightning Source LLC
LaVergne TN
LVHW092027190726

843493LV00002B/617